HOW TO ENGAGE AND STOP THE RADICALIZATION OF MUSLIMS IN THE US

Anila Ali | March 2010

What makes a young person vulnerable to recruitment by a terrorist organization? What can be done to stop it?

How to Engage and Stop the Radicalization of Muslims in the US

BY ANILA ALI

What makes young people vulnerable to recruitment by terrorist organizations? What can we do to stop radicalization of faith? To come up with an effective strategy, a solution, we must first analyze the former.

Extremism flourishes when self-image is damaged, allowing fear to become all-consuming so that divides between the haves and have-nots are perceived as

un-bridgeable. The tactics used by criminal elements to

recruit these youth to their radical ideology is similar to tactics that gangs use.

In America, young people that are moving toward radicalization are all from various socio-economic

backgrounds unlike the United Kingdom where pockets of poverty allow for terrorist breeding ground, like in Luton and Dewsbury. The American youth who are incited to radicalize are those who feel targeted and marginalized. After September 11th, racial profiling, name-calling, and stereotyping of Muslims are on the rise along with discriminatory cases against them.

Muslims as if feel they are being watched and if another tragedy like 9/11 occurs, they will face internment. Many Muslims live with this secret fear today. It is this very fear that makes them feel insecure and in turn, this fear is passed on to next of kin, the present day Muslim youth.

Muslim students, ranging from Pakistani American to Indonesian American, now feel the need to cling to their culture and religion. They feel like they need to defy authority, reinforce stereotypes, and don hijabs to redeem the self-esteem they feel they lost after 9/11. A decade ago, Muslim women were not wearing hijabs as much as they are now. Most say they do it as a reaction to Islamophobia. They say they feel "isolated." By wearing hijab, or donning a beard, as in the case of boys, they feel secure and feel a sense of pride and dignity. It is this very need to cling to their religious identity, that stops them from assimilating and integrating. Their thinking takes on an "us" verses "them" approach.

If we look at the United Kingdom, there was evident discrimination in the 70's and 80's against the Asian immigrant populations. As a result, immigrants clung hard to their archaic traditions and simply refused to assimilate. They felt they were the targets of hate crime and were "unwanted". In the case of Muslims in the UK, instead of embracing the progressive Islam, they started adhering to the dogmatic Islamic ideology practiced in much of the Muslim world. The present third, second and third generations of Muslim immigrants, are mostly conservative, unprogressive, and are fighting to establish Sharia Law in the UK. This has caused a resurgence of the 'Skin head' movement (our equivalent of the 'KKK').

We need to rebuild the shattered self-esteem of the Muslims in America. We need to make them feel like they have a stake in this country.

Some measures that need to be taken collectively by all organizations are:

1. Uplifting of the image of Muslims across the US. Media has played a key role in reinforcing Muslim stereotypes-dark skinned, bearded Muslim men and Muslim woman only in hijab or heavily covered. The media needs to cover events and people that portray Islam and Muslims as moderates.

2. Governmental Level: Empty vessels make the most noise. It seems most of the organizations that are right wing or on the cusp, get the most attention. Truth is, their following is not at all significant in the US but because they make the most noise, they muffle moderate voices. These moderate voices need to be amplified. What we must not forget is that by giving credence to such right wing thinking, we are forgetting about the millions of moderate, progressive Muslims. This group of Muslims has taken a quiet

back seat since 9/11. They feel the damage to their image has been done and that nothing can done about it. They are living honest; hard-working lives as

Americans but hesitate to voice their opinions openly. This is the silent majority that we need to engage. There are Muslim organizations that hold annual event to justify their existence but the majority of the Muslims in America are not aligned with any of these organizations. There are many other such organizations that are serving the needs of a few. We need to promote the softer side of Islam, one of flourishing arts and culture that builds the cultural, soft side of Muslims.

3. A moderate version of Islam- one that most Muslims in America follow-must be highlighted. This is the Islam that was being practiced in Iraq and Spain- an enlightened, moderate Islam. "America needs to promote a moderate Islam," William Dalrymple, "to root out extremism from its roots." This Islam is the real Islam; accepting of all religions, tolerant of others viewpoints and peaceful. In order to do that, we must establish Islamic Education Chairs,

scholarships, and encourage Americans to learn Islamic languages and cultures. It must be noted that all appointments to these centers must be screened and those chosen must be individuals who subscribe to moderate Islam. Women, especially without hijabs, should be given opportunities to head these chairs. This moderate side of Islam can be portrayed through cultural exchanges such as dance and drama troupes from various Muslim countries. Again, OIC envoy should take this initiative.

4. Another very important point to note is that the imams that are visiting our youths at university campuses must not be radicals. All Muslim clerics need to be screened and then approved for counseling on campus. In the case of the "Irvine 11", the cleric who was visiting the campus was confrontational, and instigated hate speech. Muslim clerics must abide by a code of conduct- no hate speech highlight the similarities between the religions and not the differences. Parental support groups/ community organizations can oversee the religious education and thus be aware of their children's mindset.

5. Leadership mentoring and achievement recognition of the Muslim community by the administration can play a key role in improving the civic engagement of the Muslim Americans. Organizations and individuals can be recognized annually for their role in mentoring youth and serving the community. These individuals and organizations must defy the stereotypes of Muslims- Muslim women in western clothes as opposed to women in hijab doing Interfaith- shunning of Muslim stereotypes is very important to reversing the damage done by stereotyping.

6. Regular town hall meetings with Muslims and youth to give them a forum to voice concerns, discuss, and negotiate are necessary. These youth forums will be meetings that are educational but at the same time must include entertainment and arts. Promotion of arts and culture is key to combating extremism. By promoting and enhancing the cultural side of Islam, we are invariably validating moderate Islam. Radical

thinking condemning music and arts as being haram (prohibited) can be eliminated through the promotion of Islamic art and culture and music.

7. Youth advisory committees should be set up at national and state level to work with law enforcement and intelligence agencies. The dearth in Muslim intelligence personnel is due to the distrust that exists between the Muslims and the law enforcement. This divide can be bridged when such advisory committees are functional and Muslims see that their own people are involved in keeping them safe.

8. Propaganda campaigns, plays, documentaries, movies, YouTube videos, Facebook pages, and other forms of social media can work very well if conceived with emotional appeal. Muslim Americans must see that the terrorists " have no religion" and use them as "collateral." Pro active and positive messaging of the universal message of Islam with emphasis on gender equality, moderation, and secular values of justice, equal rights, and democracy.

What we need to understand is that extremist Islam is an ideology that is a product of our own shortcomings-the Taliban is our own creation. An ideology can only be fought and counter attacked by an equally powerful ideology. The disenfranchisement of the Muslims began with Bush but can end with Obama. For that to happen, we must be proactive and foresee the simmering problems in our American Muslim communities. The Israeli-Palestinian issues have always stoked

hate and anger, the Kashmir issue the same as was evident on California campuses recently. If we don't heed the call now and take proactive measures, two years from now, may be too late. With President Obama's historic outreach speech, Muslims felt hopeful that their grievances will be redressed. Israel-Palestine issue looms like a gray cloud and the Kashmir

issue remains in the background like an imminent thundercloud. Muslims feel that the present administration is shying away from engaging Muslims in prominent positions. Muslims feel frustrated at the lack of representation in the Obama administration and divisions based on race and religion have only grown since the Invasion of Iraq.

I would propose a multi prong approach to prevent radicalizing of youth. The above strategies, individually, must be elaborated and customized, to a particular community's needs and executed as a package. The efforts need to be long term, strategic and consistent and must be professionally managed.

History of this White Paper

This white paper, based on research and work with youth and Muslims across the U.S. was submitted to The White House in 2010, to Paul Monteiro who was the former Public Engagement Advisor in the White House Office of Public Engagement. Since then, radicalization and extremism, the threat of which seemed exaggerated, have taken on a new turn, homegrown terrorism is a biggest threat to our homeland.

Overwhelming majorities of American Muslims stand with law enforcement in the fight against homegrown terrorism and radicalization and denounce terrorism. A Muslim American women's organization, American Muslim Women's Empowerment Council AMWEC, founded to give voice to Muslim women and engage them in public life and civic duty in collaboration with LAPD, counter-terrorism and FBI, has passed a resolution to work with all law enforcement agencies to fight radicalization and support the government's policy on Countering Violent Extremism, CVE. Although moderate Muslims suffered backlash from some Muslim organizations and their supporters, who did not support CVE and called it, "spying program", very contrary to the truth, they moderate Muslims, especially women continued to forge ahead with its support for CVE.

As part of this group of brave Muslim women, I thank law enforcement especially LAPD's Muslim outreach, under the leadership of Deputy Chief Michael Downing, L.A. Sheriff's Department, FBI and their leadership under Dave Bowdich for giving Muslim women the courage to elevate their voices and having a platform from where to lead.

Look up their work, and amplify their voices: www.amwec.com FB pages American Muslim Women's Empowerment Council.

Although the rate of radicalization was about 16-17 cases per year in 2010, it has now grown significantly. Muslim American organizations and a vast majority of Muslim individuals reject Islamic terrorism, and extremist ideologies.

However, radicalization has grown here in North America such as it has in the UK and Europe due to many reasons. As marginalized youth, who may be feeling abandoned by parents, community, and feeling unsuccessful at building relationships, are the prime target of recruiters. They are angry, disenfranchised and lack role models and mentors around them. They end up spending hours surfing the Internet and become the targets of radical messages. Thus, many young people who start espousing extremist views and blame US and the West for its bias in foreign policy such as the case of Israel-Palestine, actually start believing that the Western world is in conflict with Islam and behind every violent act, they see a divine, intervention of God as punishment for US foreign policy towards Israel.

The complication arises when these radicalized individuals are born U.S. citizens, such as in the case of Rizwan Malik, San Bernardino terrorist, and Omar Mateen, both U.S. citizens. For them, terrorism and murder was one way to deal with internal conflicts, such as anger, grievances, and other self-esteem issue.

Parents, friends, educators, healthcare workers, and community members can identify these cases. As an educator, I see these individuals the same way as we see 'at risk' students in a classroom. In this case however, they are 'at-risk' of radicalizing and following a radical Jihadi theory of Islam. While the threat of radicalization is real and growing, it poses a huge problem for law enforcement as when to intervene, how to intervene, and at the same time protect the civil rights of all individuals.

This is where the real challenge in combatting radicalization lies, walking the fine lie between protecting civil liberties and identifying indicators of radicalization and being able to do something about it. The only way to curtail it is through trusted partnerships with communities, law enforcement and through education. A desperate parent asked me to counsel their teen, a highly intelligent young man who was a graduate from a great liberal school. This young man was extremely angry at President Obama's decision not to intervene in Syria and US's support for Israel, note he was a South Asian Muslim who had never been outside of the US. After spending some hours talking to him, I was able to convince him that he can channel his anger in 'constructive engagement.' I suggested organizations, think tanks, and policy forums where he could learn to advocate and effect change. Because, this was done in a non-threating, unofficial, safe, and collegial way, the young man was very receptive. This is one case where parents were from a higher socio-economic standing along with being well read and vigilant. They detected the indicators of radicalization, and intervened. Many parents, who do not have good communication with their children, will not be able to intervene effectively.

Thus parents and educators must be trained to spot the indicators of extremism and radicalization just as they are taught to intervene and report cases of child abuse.

I have always advocated for inclusion of Muslim women in policy making such as the policy of countering violent extremism. But prior to that, I have been fighting to ensure that in all government advertising and training materials, Muslims are not stereotyped, that for every ten Muslim women, 6 are shown without hijab and the diversity in Muslims is highlighted and equally represented. The fallacy that a Muslim man has to have a beard and a Muslim woman has to have a hijab, has to be corrected by mainstream American media. Majority of Muslim women do not wear hijab and majority of Muslim men do not have beards. Majority of Muslims in the world are not Arabs, (less than 20% are Arabs) and majority of Muslims from South Asia have their own cultural dress code that encompasses Islamic modesty. The Mughals, who were the Muslim rulers of India for 600 years, cultivated a culture, a dress code and a way of life that is remembered by historians with nostalgia as a period of progressive, inclusive, and tolerant Islamic rule. A time when there truly was "no compulsion in Islam." Learning and education, love for arts and music, and co-existed with all religious beliefs in the Sub-Continent of

India. The increase in hijab wearing Muslim women is a direct result of the infiltration of Wahhabi ideologies in American mosques and beyond. Many of the women from non-hijab cultures will suddenly don a hijab to express their religious identity, when truly the hijab is a cultural identity. Thus giving way to a new form of discrimination in America, marginalization of non-Hijab wearing women. However, this new development must not be ignored. I have been told many a times, that I cannot represent mosques because I do not wear a hijab. I speak to aspiring women leaders across the nation and they constantly have to fight the hijab battle. My response to them is to look no further than their own grandmothers and great grandmothers for inspiration. I have a two-hundred-year history of women leaders in my family in India, who did not know the concept of 'hijab' but adorned themselves with their beautiful cultural and modest outfits such as sarees and shalwar kurtas. I have started to remind women that they must look to their enlightened ancestors. Islam was sent to an ignorant, tribal, licentious Arabia, where girls were buried alive but it was indeed, the light of Islam that stopped the girls from being buried alive.

An average American Muslim woman, educated and enjoying the privileges and rights of a free America, must not forget the enlightenment that Islam gave to Muslim women. It broke taboos and set precedence on women's rights in Islam.

The Prophet of Islam married a businesswoman, Khadija, who was twice divorced, fifteen years his senior, with children from previous marriage, a businesswoman, his boss, and she sought his hand in marriage- truly there is something to be said about women's rights in Islam 1400 years ago.

Therefore, the fight to dispel misconceptions about Muslim women and their rights in Islam is the need of the day. For, it is only through the empowerment of Muslim women and youth, through education and engagement, that we will be able to fight the extremism that has overtaken the narrative on Islam.

The next ten years are crucial for the Muslims in America and our future depends on whether we take the bull by the horn or we find scapegoats.

I say take the bull by the horn and call a spade a spade.
#ReclaimIslam
Reclaim the Islam that your grandparents followed not the one that the extremists are preaching.
-Anila Ali

Is it enough to be an American and say we love it?
I am an American and I love America. I proudly state that
I chose to become an American and when I took the oath
to protect it; I meant it.

Islam is my religion and it condemns violence against
any human being.

It seems that this introduction is not going to suffice
even in a pluralistic America. Why because today's
politics is dominated by negative narratives about
Muslims.

My fellow Americans, I want to educate you about
your neighbors- the Muslims in America. They are
diverse- they are not all Arabs and they do not all speak
Arabic. They come from China, Bangladesh, Sri Lanka,
India, Pakistan, Afghanistan, Iran, Bosnia, Russia,

Uzbekistan, Indonesia, Turkey, United Kingdom, Jordan, Somalia, Sudan, Philippines, Malaysia, you got my drift?

Majority of Muslims in America are just like any other immigrants in American, respectful, tolerant, and law abiding, living here to give their families a better life, an opportunity they did not have or they would not have immigrated to this land of equal opportunities.

Here is what may surprise you:

Majority of them do not even know what Sharia Law is and neither do they follow it. If they really wanted Sharia Law, they would have lived in Saudi Arabia, where yes, they do chop heads on Holy Days, as they follow the most archaic forms of Sharia Law. Muslims in America do not follow the Sharia Law; they follow the Constitution of the United States of America. For those who would like to follow Sharia Law, I request them to move to Saudi Arabia. As for the majority of us, we love America and our Constitution.

Also, please note, even Pakistan, doesn't follow the Sharia Law, but thanks to the Wahhabi influence from the Middle East, even they are struggling to protect the Constitution of Pakistan. When any brave soul speaks out against the Sharia Law, reformation, minority rights, respect for women, the Taliban and now a new menace to our world- the ISIS target them.

Majority of Muslims in America, have no knowledge of the concept of Taqquiya, -Muslims can deceive non-Muslims. I heard about it in Saudi Arabia (from where I thankfully escaped unharmed) and then in America, when someone asked me:

"You only pretend to be like us. You are following Taqquiya." I had to Google it.

"What? You kidding me! I am here in America to be free sister', so I do not have to lie! I must love human beings irrespective of who they are and what they believe in, that is my religion. And by the way, my parents told me that lying was a sin; that's the end of the story."

But yes, there is a minority here that may be suffering from a moral crisis; wants western comforts but does not agree with Western values. For those who do not agree with American values such as the freedoms of speech, there is an alternative, migrate to another country.

And yes the simmering questions, women's rights in Islam. Women have equal rights in Islam. (See my previous reference to the Life of the Prophet of Islam) and no, my husband does not have the right to 'beat' or 'hit' me for any reason. It is misinterpreted, yes, for reasons such as male domination and fear of women's empowerment. Education for girls is also not encouraged for the same reasons. And no, honor killings are not

Islamic and there is no basis of it in the religion, they are mad-made. And female genital mutilation has no basis in Islam although practiced in some parts of Egypt and Sudan; it is against the teachings of Islam.

Majority of Muslims are here in pursuit of happiness and economic empowerment. Whether we are gay, straight, LGBTQ or not, we must not forget that America is the bastion of Pluralism in the world. It is a country where anyone can pray to whoever and whatever he or she wish. There truly is no compulsion in religion in America and neither is there compulsion in Islam. Thus in essence, America is the greatest country to live in and if we decide to make it our home, we must love all of its values of inclusion, civil liberty and justice for all.

Below are some links to articles that have been published in various newspapers and magazines:

1. Moderate Muslim Speaks Out Against Extremism
http://www.ocregister.com/articles/muslim-649192-muslims-ali.html

2. Empowering Muslim Women
http://articles.latimes.com/2011/may/08/local/la-me-muslim-women-20110508

3. Wife Beating in Islam
http://pakistanlink.org/Commentary/2011/Sep11/02/02.HTM

4. Blasphemy Law and Islam
http://www.americanthinker.com/blog/2011/03/pakistans_infamous_blasphemy_l.html

5. On Times Square Bombing
http://www.americanthinker.com/blog/2010/05/a_pakistaniamerican_on_the_tim.html

About the author:

https://en.wikipedia.org/wiki/Anila_Ali

http://www.ocregister.com/articles/muslim-649192-muslims-ali.html

Like the page on FB:

Million American Muslims March Against Violent Extremism

The author on the panel at The White House Summit on Countering Violent Extremism, CVE, in February 2015.